A Series of Emotions

A Series of Emotions

A Collection of Short Stories and Poems

N. S.

A Message from the Author

Thank you, first and foremost, for taking the time to read this book. I wrote the following stories and poems mostly as an outlet for myself whenever I had, or had a memory of, strong emotions. It's personal in nature. It means a lot to me to have written it, and to be sharing it with you all. I hope that you enjoy it. Possibly some of you might relate to some of these feelings. That's the intention at least.

Sincerely,

N. S.

Love & Longing

<u>Enigma</u>

Oh enigma!

Let me hear the words of your heart.

Oh enigma!

Forever tormented by the infinitely vast expanse between myself and your soul.

Oh enigma!

Reveal your secrets and remove the shroud of mystery,
that I might be released from the curse of ignorance.

Oh enigma!

Unveil your mind and let me know all of you.

Oh enigma!

Oh enigma!

<u>Her</u>

The sight of her strikes a chord in my heart.
My breath falters under her piercing gaze as much as it does from the beauty of
her captivating eyes.
I am ensorcelled.

I am drawn to her like a moth to flame.
Inexorably moving towards total annihilation of myself,
so that I may become part of her.
She is fire and I seek only to burn within her.

As I gaze into the depths of the ocean of her eyes,
my attention is drawn away by the whole of her face.
She is perfect.

I could look upon her all day, every day, and never tire of it.
Looking at her, and receiving her gaze in return, feels like sitting alone in the
middle of a serene meadow.
The sounds of gentle streams babbling, and the warmth of the sun
smiling down through the canopy.

And her smile,

oh, her smile makes me weak.

I not only see, but can *feel* her smile.

Coyness, mischief, playfulness, and confidence.

The curvature of her lips,

the way her teeth slightly show,

I am hopelessly entranced once more.

But there is more still,

even though I could not fathom her being more beautiful,

there is more.

Her hair, framed so neatly about her jaw,

ending just below her face,

has a life of its own.

It parts in the perfect way no matter how she turns.

It is silken and shines brighter than any light.

I close my eyes momentarily, and reopen them,

just to see her anew once more.

Her beauty,

her radiance that brightens my otherwise dreary existence.

She fills me with exuberance,

just by allowing me to watch her.

With my sight renewed,

I notice how the gentle curve of her face,

from her high cheekbones to her smooth jaw

to her slender chin,

only serves to heighten every other piece of the perfection that is her.

Her skin glows like the moon,
smoother than marble.
Rosiness blushes across her cheeks,
accentuating the light peach tone of her skin.

I am dumbfounded.
Standing here before her in awe.
Aphrodite herself could come to me
and she would be *nothing*
compared to the vision before me.

Let me be in this state forever.
Let me stay here to gaze upon her, nothing else matters.
I wish for eternity to find me.
Her beauty is all I need.
She is all I need.

But, like all things, the joy of her is fleeting.
The longer I look, the hazier her visage becomes.
I frantically try to maintain my focus,
to stay here,
to keep my sight of her intact.
The image only hastens to dissipate,
and I groan in anguish.

My eyes come open slowly, and I stare up into the dim light of dawn.
I suppress the urge to rage at my fantasy, and rise from slumber.
I know I'll never see her again,
I can only hope the memory of her remains.

<u>Unrequited</u>

These feeble words do not adequately express the awe I feel as I look at her
beauty.

She intrigues and attracts me so;
much like the moon is attracted to the sun.
Chasing it blindly across the night and day,
seeking only to share in its warmth and light.

But like the moon,
I am unable to reach her.
The pain I feel at knowing
that despite sharing the same sky,
we shall never truly meet,
is nigh unbearable.
Even if I were to eclipse her radiance,
it would only serve to deny others their chance in the sun.

I shall never know her,
and although the thought of this is intolerable,
I must endure still.
For even though we cannot be as one,

I can still look upon her, and steal what joy I can at the sight of her.

<u>Perfect</u>

Perfection: the condition, state, or quality of being free
or as free as possible from all flaws or defects.

She is the very definition.

My heart flutters to and fro
in an endless dance of joy at the mere thought of her.

If I could,
I would harness the whole of the cosmos
in barter for a single smile from her.

Words truly fail me.

Elation abounds.

Thoughtlessly and without effort,
my love for her surpasses the self imposed limitations I have

I am hopelessly
and endlessly
trapped in her,
and my satisfaction in this couldn't be greater

She is beyond compare

Nothing,
not the heavens
nor the gods themselves
could decry the virtue of my devotion

She completes that which was left barren

She is the very definition of love,
and I am inundated in the storm of my emotions

I love her

Without shame

Without restraint

Without bias, or judgment, or expectation

Love

My dearest, my most treasured

I love you

<u>Yearning</u>

As I wandered the expansive wastes, I heard it. A small, quiet, sound. Akin to the far off lilting howl of some sorrowful beast. But it couldn't be so. There was nothing here. There never had been, and never would be. Despite this, the sound invaded.

I was startled to say the least. In my eons of roaming, not once had something ever occurred beyond the earth below my feet shifting under the weight of my steps. I had given up hope long ago of ever breaking free of my solitary trudge onward into infinity.

Yet, as if to mock me, this sound came. The sound was simultaneously haunting, beautiful, mournful, and wistful. The volume and intensity of the sound built as I pondered its source. I frantically searched the horizon for a sign, but, as ever, there were no changes; no indication of its origin.

The sound was greater than anything I'd ever experienced. I felt it through the core of my being; and at once I felt this must be how I finally meet my end, my respite, my solace.

As the crescendo peaked, the sound suddenly ceased. I was left wanting for but a moment, before a blinding flash of light erupted across the barren landscape. The light dissipated from the periphery of my vision until a lone ray of luminescence remained upon the horizon.

With renewed purpose, I sought this new experience. With vigor and haste I'd not known for millennia, I sprinted across the land; and as I drew near, I saw something within the light. Someone in the light.

I ran faster and faster. The shape became more distinct. Even within the purity of this light, it was a being more radiant than anything else. Anything I'd ever known or conceived.

I arrived, and before me was a woman bathed in pale light. I was in awe of her. I knew her. I'd never met her, but my soul knew her. Without trepidation I reached my hand out to hers, and as my fingertips grazed hers, I saw her eyelids flutter and slowly open. Her gaze fell upon me. Seeing me again, and for the first time.

She knew me. All of me, down to my core. As she came fully alive I could feel her warmth penetrate me. Her arms wrapped me up into her, and I wept openly. Tears of joy flowed for finally being able to be with her, tears of anguish for knowing this was our end, and frustration at the futility of our efforts. All my life, all my pain, all my efforts and struggles were for this singular moment; and just like that, it was over. The woman faded from around me, the light dimmed and again I was left hollow, and alone.

I sat. . . For the first time in my existence, I sat. No tears would come, despite my sorrow. I could not rage, despite my fury. I was alone again.

Time passed. . . I could no longer remember her warmth, so I stood.

More time passed. . . I could no longer remember her gaze, so I took a step.

At last, enough time passed that I could no longer remember her. I breathed deeply, and continued on my endless journey through the expansive wastes.

As I trudged onward, suddenly there was a sound. A small, quiet sound. . .

Loneliness & Despair

<u>Hollow</u>

Hollow.
Hollow throughout and within.
Emptiness bears down on me.
I seek endlessly.
I am the sole proprietor of this fate.
My own, my terminus.

It is a curse.
This flagging ship carries on with no passengers,
no crew,
only myself as it's captain.
Every port I seek,
every port is found wanting.

I seek not for the adventure,
or the riches,
only the comfort of knowing
I will no longer be the only one to man this vessel.
The emptiness pervades my decks eternally
as I'm adrift without course.

A course to nowhere.
Everywhere is the destination, when there is none.
The myriad lands I see stretched before me fail to be home for me,
and my wandering continues.
The horizon brings no solace,
only new torment and continued anguish.

None shall suffer me,
and I know it is right to do so.
Who would be one to join a captain
on his voyage into the depths of eternity?
No wise one would do so.
Joining one in the abyss is folley.
No, it is right to leave me,
abandoned to fate.

I continue, in perpetuity, on my journey.
My fate.
My curse.
Forever seeking.

I will continue until the end, until this ship fails me.
It is a captain's duty.
It is only the smallest hope that holds me to this,
but that is all I need.
One day,
perhaps.
One day.

Continue.
Continue ever onward,
this journey through solitude.
Tomorrow is a new day,
a new port,
and a new chance.
Will my fate be reconciled?
Only tomorrow will I know.

<u>Outside</u>

It sits before me, beckoning me.

I look into it,
and inside, I can sense warmth,
joy,
playfulness,
and community.

I reach inside it,
I want to obtain the same feelings.
But as I reach inside,
the feelings vanish.
I desperately long for those feelings.
So I reach into it again.
Again the feelings vanish.
I step back now and watch as the feelings return,
and I admire them.

I grab it,
I get as close to it as I can,
and hold it dear to me.
Every time I try to reach in,
the feelings still vanish.
But if I get this close,
if I bring myself to the point just before I cross the threshold,
I can almost feel them.

Even this is enough,
even this will sate me.
I hold it to me for a time,
and as the hours grow longer,
so too does the desire to be one with it.

But I know better,
if I want to be allowed even this much sensation,
I must resist.

I've grown mournful now.
My desire has exceeded my capacity to tolerate.
I hate myself for being unable to join with it.

I am saddened, but I must leave it behind.
I move away, and it is none the wiser.
I was never there to begin with,
I didn't know how to be.

<u>Desperate</u>

As the emptiness begins to take hold, I try desperately to fill the void.

I am afraid.

I seek companionship from others to beat back the unending loneliness that is within me to no avail.

I try to escape into alternative realities of man's creation without success.

The emptiness grows still.

I am terrified.

I plead for an ending to my sorrow
and the hollow comforts I repeatedly use
in a weak attempt to hide from myself.

The emptiness consumes me.

I am no longer.

<u>Filth</u>

Like the swine that wallows in the mud,
I rut about in the filth of my own making.

Those that perceive me take note of my pitiable behavior,
and whilst they seek to instruct me on how to remain clean
they shall not take up the burden of assistance.

I try to rise out of the muck
and find myself mired in the dregs of circumstance.

Time and again I try,
a stain cleansed here,
a splotch polished away there.
It is fruitless,
as the efforts only bring greater notice to the rest of the detritus.

Would that the waters of hope saw fit to wash over and invigorate me
so that I could be free of this.

But it is a vain wish.
I seem only able to wade in the bog.
The ones from before that sought to instruct me have all gone now,
I am alone with the rest of the swine.

I cannot bear the stench of myself any longer.
I shut off my mind, and let myself move on base instinct alone,
rooting through the filth
for whatever morsels I can find
to sustain me.

I subsist
in this low place, forever.

<u>Alone</u>

I cannot feel them.
They are so near, but I do not see them.
I long for their touch,
but it doesn't arrive.
I retreat into the void of my soul.

They are there,
offering unattainable comfort.
I try again to go to them, but I am pulled back out of reach.
I see the darkness wrapped around me,
dragging me away.
I am being smothered by the abyss.

They cry out for me,
the sound muffles
as the inky black of my soul
swallows me whole.
I am afraid.
I want to escape.
I frantically flail around for anything.
Anything that can pull me out of this pit.

My hands gain no purchase,
and I am borne off deeper into solitude.
I weep and resign myself to my fate.

The void takes me into its arms and embraces me.
I howl in despair and anguish.
I cannot leave.
I accept it.
I am alone.
They are too far away now to save me.
If only I could have reached them.
If only.

<u>Stay</u>

Do you need me?

I need you.

Do you want me to stay?

Yes I do.

I cannot hear your words.

I'm right here, don't go.

I'm in so much pain, I cannot bear it any longer.

Please, don't make me miss you so.

I'm sorry I can't stay anymore.

Wait, don't go, I'm here.

Goodbye.

My heart aches, I wish you were still near.

<u>Anyone</u>

Help, help.

I'm drowning in my sorrow and pain.

I reach out desperately for anyone,
anything,
to pull me from this ocean of torment.

Nothing is working,
nothing is bringing me above sea level.

Help, help.

I don't want to give up,
but my arms are so tired from treading water.

My lungs are struggling for air
as I fight against the currents
that continuously try to bring me under.

These words serve as my life raft,
and they have a hole.

Help, help.

Please, anyone.

Please, anything.

Please, see me drowning.

Don't let me sink.

Don't let me drown.

Help, help.

Anger & Determination

<u>Soar</u>

I was soaring in the skies overhead, freedom and limitless opportunity before me, and then I saw you. You, so far below me, looking forlorn. Your sadness at being grounded called to me. I descended to meet you, hoping to lift you up.

We spoke, and your shackles holding you down were made apparent. I tried my hardest. I did my best to remove your shackles, one by one. And when you were finally free, we rose to the sky. It was bliss. I thought.

We pushed forward endlessly, weaving and ducking through storms and fair weather alike. I felt you beside me all the way, and felt better for it. But as we went farther, I noticed you falling back. I slowed myself, I wanted to be with you all the way. But you slowed too much, and began falling from the sky.

I dove to meet you as you crashed to the ground. Your shackles had returned, and were more restrictive than ever. I again tried to help. I began removing shackles, taking them onto myself. But you refused me. You put the burden of your shackles upon me, even while refusing to remove any yourself.

Finally, when I was burdened to the earth, another came along and offered you their hand. At the sight of them, you transferred your shackles, all your burdens, to me and escaped with them. You left me and all your burdens behind without remorse. I watched through tearstained eyes. Rage filled me with your betrayal. I turned to my new shackles and I saw them for what they were.

My shackles, your shackles given to me, were your memories, your responsibility, your helplessness, and your guilt. The fact you turned away from them so easily with another, pained me more. I accepted all the pain, all the frustration, all the anger borne by these chains. It flooded within me, and faded.

I am in the skies once more, and I proudly bear the scars from the restraints you bound me with. But whenever I see you, they heat to an excruciating level. And when I see you fly with another, the one who took you away from your burden, the pain and hate becomes unbearable.

But I must endure, and fly further, and further into the horizon.

<u>Fury</u>

The heat inside me is full to bursting,
the atmosphere cowers and quakes before me.
My incandescent anger courses through the earth
and causes the molten core of terra to shudder.
I am rage incarnate,
my fury will not be quenched.

My disdain for all things is unbound.
With every step the ground bursts and bubbles beneath me.
I have a single thought,
a sole purpose.
I will reach my destination,
even though it will destroy me.
But my fury has no other purpose
but to eliminate its source.

I stomp towards the enemy.
The air around me is plasma,
crackling across my skin and scarring me.
The pain is a distant thought.
Nothing and no one can stop me.

I arrive.

In a rush of emotions,
I unleash all my might upon them.
All the anguish,
torment,
hate,
fury,
and suffering
I have borne is unbridled
and cascades across the landscape.
The land is forever changed
and a sea of fire, molten rock, ash, and soot are born.
I look upon my work with satisfaction,
and the fury subsides.
The rage inside me cools,
but does not leave.

As I move away
I know I am forever changed.
Nothing in this universe will bring me succor once more.
Though the origin of hate has been annihilated,
it is too late.
Fury is who I am become,
and fury is what I shall bring to all.

I shall not suffer the pains of the past again,
and all who do not stand aside me
shall be put to the flame.

<u>Endure</u>

Piece by piece I am torn.
Parts of me leave while others stay,
and I am left incomplete.
As I am rent asunder, I ponder my fate.
My own decisions and indecision led me down this path.

I reminisce of the time I was whole fondly,
and wonder if I shall be able to return to that time one day.
I assume it is so,
since it is the natural state of being for me.
Even still, I can feel the phantom pain of my missing parts,
and mourn their loss.

The pain is a dull ache,
throbbing and acting as a constant reminder of what I lost.
It occasionally overwhelms me,
and I double over and cry out for release from it.
But then it subsides,
and I am left as I was before.

Broken,

wounded,

lame.

I am made to realize my inadequacy with every hurdle

I was able to easily overcome

when I was complete.

I struggle against that which threatens to smother me.

Dogged determination,

inescapable responsibility,

and willpower

are the only things that drive me to continue.

I am spiteful of my predicament,

but know that I am to blame

as much as that which betrayed me.

I will continue onwards

and find within

the ways to rebuild myself anew.

Borrowing from all my past and future experiences

to form a new whole being.

A renewed self

that does not rely on the parts borrowed

from those who would seek to act for their own benefit

when times are difficult.

A renewed self

that can be a pillar

for those who would need strength during times of sorrow and anguish.

A person unto their own,

standing firm amid the turbulent flow of life.

The pain will not subside
until I am once again whole.
It will be the continuous catalyst for change
that makes me greater than before.
I welcome the pain,
and its presence motivates me.
Until the day that all that is missing has been replaced
and been remade stronger.
And should the pain persist,
then it too shall be made part of me.

I shall endure.

Frustration & Weakness

<u>Futile</u>

My mind roils with tumultuous nonsense

The solace I crave from my own stream of consciousness fails to find me.

I am lost amidst the ebb and flow of an endless sea of thoughts and desires.

Have mercy on me, my mind. Silence, I say.

Let me rest, and give me peace.

I grasp at the words as they come and go and commit them to permanence on page.

It is a vain attempt to expend the energies that drive my disarrayed visions.

My attempts to gain serenity are for naught, and I drown in chaos.

Unending, ceaseless thought torments me.

I shall continue, and hope that calm will come.

Someday.

<u>Struggle</u>

The noise in my mind grows.
A small drumbeat steadily increases into a pounding
that thrums through my core.
I tense and resist to the best of my ability,
but it seems for naught.
I cannot escape from myself and the agony I feel.

I know the answer,
I know how to soothe this pain.
The easement to my torment,
the escape from my agony.

The nagging continues and I almost relent.
Even still,
I hold fast.
I know this pain is momentary.
I can weather the storm.

The pain subsides and I relax.
The relief I feel from enduring is a momentary respite.
I know that soon again the torture will resume.

I cannot succumb.

I am assaulted again.

It's excruciating.
I cannot bear it.
I must.

I beg for relief.
It is within reach.
I stretch out to grasp the antidote to my anguish.
I am there.
I falter, I know it is folly.
I must not.
It will subside,
it always does.

The intensity increases.
I am pleading with myself.
Please, don't.
Please, do it.
I wrench myself away
only to be closer than ever.

I relent.
I have failed.
Sweet, sweet failure.
I take my antidote,
the poison fills me.

I am ashamed.
I am sublime.
The strength I lack is made apparent.
I relish in weakness.

The poison leaves me,
and I feel empty and wanting.
My core cries out.
I know the agony will return.
I will be stronger,
I hope.

The pain returns, and my struggle rages anew.

<u>Starving</u>

An emptiness gnaws and nags at me

A void begging to be filled

Without shame I fill myself full,
but the lonely feeling inside only grows

I fill myself again,
only to find I'm no longer able to be full

Desperately seeking the satisfaction of completion,
I fervently consume everything in sight

The hollow inside me only grows,
and I no longer have any capacity for anything
outside of devouring whatever lies before me

I lament my inability to feel what once was known so well,
and weep as I continuously chase after it

Hunger drives and consumes me. I am lost to it.

<u>Lust</u>

Heat

Burning,
raging inside me

Flames lick
and crawl over my skin

The inferno kisses me all over
as I struggle to contain it

I am ablaze

Desire bursting throughout my form,
made manifest

As I gaze outward and see the object of my desire,
I unleash myself

Unbridled,
emboldened

The heat dictates my actions,
and dominates my mind

For better or worse,
I pursue my prey

Unquenchable

I am a wildfire

crackling,
spitting my heat all over
in the hopes to spread

I am ceaseless in my quest for the one that will soothe my rampant flames.

Indolent

Heaviness, the air is thicker than water.

Weight bears down without remorse,
I know I must rouse myself, but cannot

I look around and see the labors I am due to perform

I approach responsibility,
and in its face I shirk away

I promise I will accomplish these tasks

Later

I look beyond and see the beauty of the world fading in the distance,
falling away to disease and blight.

But I am here now,
in this bountiful land.

I turn away,
my thoughts will return to this problem

Another time

Again and again the world begs me to act
Again and again I am unable to

I am drowning in purpose

I am tired

Rest,
I will do it after I rest

A lie

Apathy & Resignation

<u>Weightless Pt.1</u>

Weightless. That is the feeling I have when I become conscious. I move my arms and feel resistance as I do. I move my legs and the same resistance. I open my eyes and the world around me is distorted.

I turn my head in all directions and see nothing. There is a dim light throughout that allows me to see how truly empty this place is.

As my head turns below I see the light being swallowed by an endless void. Above I see a shifting surface refracting the light in various directions, perpetually moving in seemingly random ways.

I am underwater. I am unsure how I arrived here, or why I am here, but my first instinct upon discovering my predicament is to reach the surface. I begin swimming upward. The surface grows clearer and larger in my vision as I get closer to my goal.

I am moments away from breaking the tension of the water, I can see the end now. The water thickens, and the resistance I feel when I'm swimming is impossible to overcome. I can no longer make progress, mere inches from my goal and I am stalled.

I struggle mightily. The more I struggle, the more I fight, the harder the water pushes me down. I am no longer near the surface. This prison pulls me down further and further.

I am panicking and raging against the tide as it tears me further away from my destination. I am furious, but every attempt to make progress is met by an even harsher rebuke. This ocean is less water now, and more a swamp. A mire I am unable to traverse.

The darkness around me is such that I can only barely see the light of the surface anymore. In vain, I continue trying to reach the light, instead I only get pulled further down into the abyss.

My attempts to free myself only worsen my situation. I can no longer see the light. I realize I haven't taken a breath at all, and the realization that I haven't breathed, and that I cannot because I am underwater, causes a new wave of panic. I look desperately for anything to keep from drowning. There is nothing. Against my will, my panicked mind and body inhale deeply.

The liquid pours into my throat and lungs. I cannot escape. I despair at my demise. I was so close, and now this place will be my end. The liquid chills and burns as it enters my body. I feel indescribable pain as I accept my fate. I weep, and succumb.

Throughout my whole drowning I had still been awake, I had still been desperately seeking the light. But now, at the end, I close my eyes. As my eyelids droop lower, one last look towards the surface reveals the light once more. The faintest, slightest glimmer. I smile, and am thankful for the final send off.

I still feel sorrow, but I am calm now. I accept this fate. All my struggles resulted in nothing gained. All my attempts at progress were thwarted by my surroundings. There was nothing my efforts accomplished. I rest now. I feel no more pain. Numbness overwhelms me. I am apathetic to it all. I smile once more. It is time, I go now.

<u>Safe</u>

Listlessness falls upon me.
I no longer feel the zeal I once did towards these activities.
I continue my monotonous tasks indefinitely,
waiting for the time to come that I am no longer required.

My only refuge,
the words I place upon the page.
I bide my time
and eagerly await the dull existence I am currently experiencing to be over.
Time slows and my thoughts wander.
Must I always be doing this?
Is this required for happiness?
Does any of it really matter?
Can I be something more?

I banish the wayward thoughts and continue on with my duties.
This is safe.
This is known.
No risk, no harm.
But how I long for fulfillment.
A small price to pay for security, I convince myself.

The time for the end draws nearer,

and drags on endlessly.

I am but a footnote in a single book of this vast library.

The smallest cog in the grand machine.

Were I to be removed I would easily be replaced. There is no value in this.

No pride.

I simply do what must be done,

and continue in perpetuity

until they see fit to make me grand,

or remove me.

Nothing here is of my own accord.

There is comfort in its mindlessness.

Still, it is safe.

It is known.

A small price to pay for security, I convince myself once more.

I am on the precipice of freedom now.

Time stands still and mocks me.

As if to firmly impress upon me the permanence of my position here,

and etch upon me that I am owned.

Time is letting me know that I am its prisoner,

and in turn their prisoner.

I cannot escape.

I long for my freedom.

I could leave at any time, but would forsake my security.

But I will not leave.
It is safe,
it is known.
A small price to pay for security, I can hardly convince myself.

Finally, the hour passes, and I am free.
With joyous rapture, I leap from my cage
and rush towards my happiness and light.
I'm no longer shackled
by those who would see me run down into the earth and trodden upon.
I move with renewed vigor.
I enjoy my freedom to its fullest.
There is nothing to hold me back.

But as I frolic, a loud noise blares across the sky to my ears.
The all too familiar klaxon of the alarm brings me down from my ecstasy.
I know this means my freedom is done.
I am to return to my tasks.
I turn back towards my cage.
I stop,
and turn again, back to the open horizon.
I long for my freedom.
Nothing is stopping me, I can take it.
But lurking beyond this light I know there is darkness.
A terrible darkness
that threatens to smother me without the support of my cage
and the protection it provides.
I am no fool.
I will seek protection.

I return to my cage,
resume my tasks,
and lose my vigor.

But it is okay.
It is safe.
It is known.
A small price to pay for security, I know.

<u>Nothing</u>

I close my eyes so I don't have to see.

Sight has become a tiresome chore that only serves to enhance the dreariness of
my outlook.
But as I lay quietly,
my breath coming and going at an even tempo,
I am assailed by unwanted images and thoughts.

Memories and regrets.
Anguish and anger
confound me with their presence,
so I open my eyes again
to escape the emotions.
It is little comfort.

Before me is a fertile land, filled with opportunity and wonder.
It may as well be a barren landscape.
I harbor no desire for this place, no ambition to pursue.

I am a husk of myself.

My empty, lifeless eyes stare outward with disdain for existence.

Curse this land and those that walk on it.

Let it be trodden upon until nought is left but dust.

I close my eyes, and again the sorrow and hatred creep in.

I cannot obtain respite.

I am trapped in a cycle of dream and reality

that heightens my frustrations endlessly.

Let the wastes have me and my soul.

For nothing but the wastes are here for me faithfully.

Such that I was made from nothing,

Such that I am nothing,

And nothing shall I remain.

<u>Fading</u>

The mask cracks and falls away.
Behind the veneered smile is the face of despair, more apparent than ever.

The listless, lifeless eyes shift about, seeking new hope.

There is none.

A wry smile cracks the lips, comfort in the lack thereof.

Understanding of their place.
Settled and worn down from all that life encompasses.
Weary from the falsehoods.
Jaded from the endless pursuit of peace without success.

Alone.

Lost.

Fading away.

They meet their end.

<u>Comfort</u>

A dull ache rattles through my bones.

I am weary.

I struggle to upright myself from my prone posture,
as the gravity of everything plunges down on me.

Every movement is agony,
as my body shrieks and wails in protest.

As I come about, I look back and see the inviting comfort of my resting place.

It tempts and seduces me.

I can hear it calling out to me with its siren tones.

"Return to me. Here there is no pain, no laborious tasks, no anguish. Only comfort.
Only shelter from the storm."

I falter.

I know to succumb to its temptation
means only greater torment when next I must arise.

Oh,
but how I long for its embrace.

How I long to flee my weariness and pain.

How I long to postpone the inevitable decay.

I attempt to turn away,
but the effort drains so.
I cannot resist.

I slowly lay myself back into the sweet, downy softness of its soothing arms.

The guilt and shame I feel for giving in
is overcome by the numbing warmth.

I cannot escape.

I don't want to escape.

<u>Bog</u>

I groan and sigh deeply as I trudge through the muck about my legs.
I am repugnant and repulsive.
I see glimpses of my reflection and cringe,
quickly stepping on my own face to obscure the image
so that I may tolerate my own self further.

Every step I take
brings me further from the last mistake,
and closer to the next.
I tread carefully, attempting vainly
to avoid obstacles
only to unwittingly crash into another.

The splash I create as I flounce into a deeper filth,
droplets arcing and flying around me,
reverberate back into
and then outward from me.
My image distorts
and my heinous appearance grows more grotesque.
I retreat inward from the increasingly distressing event.

I wait a time for the pool of inky black waste to calm,
for the ripples to subside,
and once they do I wade out once more.

I do not know where I am going,
a singular direction pulls me,
calls to me,
and I listen.
Many times I must hide from myself
and wait for waves to subside,
and each time I become a little less willing to continue.

A little more jaded.

A little more defeated.

Finally, I stop.
I no longer try to continue.
The little motivation that drove me,
urged me onward,
has vanished.

I rest,
and the swamp consumes me.

<u>Passivity</u>

Rain falls
The heavens roar in defiance

I am unaffected

Day breaks,
clouds part
Beauty surrounds me,
a renewed earth

I am nonplussed

Night falls
The enigmatic moon sheds light on terrifying darkness
the deepest corners hide wonders
and promise adventure
in equal amounts to their peril

I am unfazed

The world shatters,
and the cosmos rend themselves apart

Even still, I am unmoved

My indifference endures
and rules over all of me

Peace & Acceptance

<u>Warmth</u>

My eyes were closed,
but I could still see the intense light shining through.
I dared not open them
for fear of being stricken blind.
I wanted to so badly,
but I could not do it.

The light grew in intensity, accompanied by heat now.
It was not uncomfortable, in fact the opposite.
But the feelings it was trying to impart in me
we're not known to me.
I panicked and turned away.

Even with my back to the radiant warmth,
I could feel it reaching out
and caressing me softly.
I shivered at its touch,
unaccustomed to the comfort and relief that washed over me.
I retreated.
Further and further I sought escape.
But it would not relent.

Soon I was enveloped completely.
I fought against the pleasant sensations it brought to me.
This new thing was terrifying.
I did not understand what was being done to me.

I thrashed violently,
I cursed,
I bit and kicked,
I pleaded for it to stop.
But the warmth was patient,
kind,
and understanding.
It endured the tantrum I threw
and only sought to provide more joy to me.

I ceased my struggle.
The futility of it drained me, and left me hollow.
But this was exactly what was needed,
the warmth rushed into and filled me.
I sighed in contentment.
All the pain and sorrow I'd borne
were a distant memory now.

I opened my eyes.

Even in my current state, I had expected the light to be harsh,
as it had been with my eyes closed.
But instead, all around me was a gentle amber hue.
Like an endless field of grain on a sunny day.
I realized now, that the harsh intensity of the light
was not to ward me from seeing,
but to admonish me for blinding myself.
As if to say *"You shall see me even in your darkest places."*

Peace was brought into me.
I was serene.
There was no fear.
No doubt that the warmth would ever leave.
As I floated in this place,
I let myself close my eyes again.
I drifted off into a well overdue rest.
And my consciousness left, happiness engraved upon it.

<u>Strong</u>

My heart leaps when I catch sight of them once more.
Energy pulses throughout my body, into my limbs, and up to my brain.
A rush of pleasure overwhelms me, and I reach toward them.

As they turn to see me and smile,
I practically stumble over myself.
Even just their acknowledgement of my existence
is enough for me to banish the torment and anguish from my soul.

I chase.

Frantically, I chase.

But as I advance, the distance only grows.

Their smile fades,
the amusement of my presence is no longer enough to sate them.

Even still, I pursue them.
I reach and scramble to them.
Faster and faster,
until I am at my utmost limit.
But they are already out of sight.

The despair creeps back in and forms a haze around me.
I listlessly meander through the fog.
Hopelessness and loneliness,
my oldest friends,
appear and walk beside me again.
And as I walk,
I surrender to the emptiness within.

I know now that I'm not meant for more than this.
I know that escape from my companions is impossible.
Despite my best efforts to shake them off.
I run,
I hide,
I cry out for assistance and sanctuary.
And no matter what, my compatriots are right next to me.

Acceptance that I'll never break free
from my long time companions becomes a comfort.
I steel myself against the world,
and move forward.
Even with no clear direction, I move now with purpose.
My steps, once heavy with grief,
now lighten.

Vigor returns, and my malaise fades.

The air around me thins,
and I see my oldest and truest friends behind me.
They smile,
somehow still sorrowful even with their smiles.
The fog is with them.

I stand for a moment,
looking back on where I'd come from.
Looking back at them.
A simple nod from me to them.
My only acknowledgement that
without them I'd never know the joy that I once did.
Acknowledgement that thanks to them,
I learned to be joyful with myself.

They,
who were with me at birth,
and will be with me at death.
They,
who brought me to my lowest,
so I could find bliss at my highest.
They,
who showed me the way to happiness.

I turn away.
Though they're always with me,
I know that I can overcome them now,
with the strength they gave me.

Thank you my loneliness

Thank you my hopelessness

You have made me strong

Joy & Hope

Weightless Pt.2

I am alive. I do not know how, but I am. My eyes open again. I am shocked to find myself where I'd started when I'd first come to consciousness. Miraculously, I am back near the surface. I am wary.

I know now. I know this world will try to end me. I know my struggles will be for naught. I know my efforts will be unrewarded. Still, I know I must try again. So I go.

I try, once more. I swim upwards. I can feel the resistance coming on sooner. I do not falter, I do not panic. I continue on my way, evenly pacing myself. I feel different than before. Fierce and determined, I stubbornly continue.

The weight of the quagmire is extreme. Despite this, I do not feel hopeless like I did before. The progress is slow, but I can feel I am still advancing.

I am now closer than ever to the surface. My fingers are there. I feel the tips scrape the surface. I am elated. Another stroke. My hands break the tension.

All at once the swamp-like ocean around me falls away. I am weightless again, zero resistance. The light disperses and condenses radically. Millions upon millions of stars manifest around me in all directions. I am in the heavens.

I gaze at the cosmos before me in awe. All this beauty, all the mystery, the universe unfolding before. It was always here. The quagmire I'd struggled with was nowhere to be found, and I realized now that it never truly was there.

I smile. Contentment and happiness are finally within me. I feel a warmth throughout my being. There is a light that grows in the space around me. I look around and see no source. I look to myself and see I am shining bright. Brighter than anything else I can see. I am a beacon.

With a sense of ecstasy, I race off into the cosmos to share my newfound light with any, and all who would see. I am the brightness that shines in the dark. I shall illuminate the path for all others trapped in their own quagmire.

<u>Happy</u>

Elation.
Throughout every fiber of my being
joy rushes about.
I am energized by mutual acceptance
and reciprocated emotion.
My body feels light and I soar.

I climb to the highest I can go
and let myself feel the winds rush past me.
The sky can barely contain me as I speed past the sound barrier.

I accelerate faster and faster still.
The horizon distorts
and bright colors dance in front of me.
I dive deep into their flow
and bathe amongst the torrent.

All the colors within the spectrum of light flow into me
and I shine brighter for it.
I am content,
ecstatic,
relieved.
I dance amongst the cosmos and relish in the delight I feel.

I am happy.

<u>Journey</u>

I'm walking in absolute darkness and profound silence. I am breathing, but there is no sound, only the sensation of air filling and then escaping my lungs. The ground below me is cool, and I am aware that I have bare feet. I look down, but the darkness enveloping me is such that I cannot see myself. I bring my hand up to within inches of my face, it too is hidden from me. I am suffocating in this darkness, and panic begins to take hold. Despite this, I continue forward.

Suddenly, a light diffuses through the space. A distant speck on the horizon grows into an all encompassing, blinding white. I look to myself once more and I am whole again. I stand bare, fully laid open to the light, exposed, vulnerable.

My surroundings are seamless, there is no defined horizon, no ceiling, no floor. My perspective of myself in this space distorts as I become aware that I am walking on nothing. At this revelation, suddenly I am falling.

Panic sets in again as the feeling of free falling intensifies. The speed building as I continue plummeting through this white abyss is nauseating. There is nothing around that I can use as a point of reference to help understand the speed of my descent, but my body knows when I have reached terminal velocity. The fear of death upon my impact begins to course wildly through every fiber of my being. But a far greater fear begins to fester in the corners of my mind.

What if I never stop? What if this maddening feeling continues on forever? A sense of dread permeates throughout me and my mind races. I just want it to stop.

I am falling,

I am now accustomed to the sensation and have begun to wonder just how long I will be in this state. A feeling of seconds dragging into minutes, into hours passes through me, and I've become numb to it.

A change occurs, my body recognizes that I am slowing now. It is both unexpected and welcome that my pace is gradually reducing instead of a sudden end to it all, relief washes over me.

More time passes and I am now floating still. There is no change to the white abyss, no floor, no ceiling, no horizon. There is only the endless expanse, and myself.

I am able to move, but see little point in doing so now. Everything is the same. I'm alone with my thoughts. How long have I been here? How do I leave? Is there more to see? Why am I here? Why am I alone? How did I get here? Who am I? My thoughts grow more complex the longer I am here. I hadn't even thought of anything until this moment.

I try to reach into my mind for more information, and return with nothing. I know nothing, I feel nothing, I am nothing. But how can this be true if I'm having these thoughts? Where do these words and ideas originate from? How do I even have a concept of words and the capacity to question my existence?

I am drowning in my thoughts. The sound of my own mind is deafening. In the midst of my existential crisis something changes. Miraculously, I see something off in the distance, a small speck of something. I begin to move towards it, faster and faster I race. But the distance never decreases. I am determined, I push myself to the upper limit of how fast I can go. But even still, the speck is unattainable. I begin losing hope, defeat settling upon my shoulders. I turn away.

But the speck persists. As I turn, it turns with me, in the same place no matter how I try to avoid it. I close my eyes, trying to banish the hope it represents, but I can feel it. I can feel it boring into me, nagging me to continue. So I continue.

I trudge onward towards the distant smudge, unsure why I am continuing despite the futility of doing so. I feel an emptiness within me growing, and almost as quickly as it appeared, the stain on this white hell dissipates and vanishes. In its place a growing mire of various grays starts to invade my sight. The formlessness of this place is broken up by the smokelike expansion of this new experience. I realize that alongside the expansion of this haze, the noise within my mind grows. Soon the once white void is a murky shifting expanse of smoke. The noise in my head is too loud to bear.

I scream out in terror, frustration, anguish, despair, and contempt for my predicament. I cannot even hear myself over the roar of my mind. I see and feel the smoke around me drawing closer, until the ripples and waves of it are caressing my skin. I feel it invade my lungs, and taste it on my tongue. It feels both cold and hot at once as it dances across my body. I cry out again, but still hear nothing. I begin sobbing, wanting for it all to stop. I close my eyes again, praying for mercy from myself and this place.

In the midst of my sorrow, there is a sound. It is quiet and hard to discern, but I am able to focus on it briefly. I pursue this new sensation with all the strength I can muster, and eventually I am able to hear the sound freely. A soothing melody calms me, and quiets my thoughts. A lullaby specifically for the chaos of my mind. I relax and close my eyes. I feel the space around me, expanding my consciousness throughout this vast infinity. My despair at my inability to obtain the hope that previously eluded me fades, and I am inundated with feelings of elation and peace. The warmth in my heart overflows, and I let my feelings explode forth into this space.

My eyes open, and before me now is a cacophony of color. Shades of blue, green, violet, red, orange and yellow spiral and shift endlessly in my view, penetrating my core. The various hues swirl about and dance across my vision. I look down to myself and see that this is the once gray smoke. It now imparts a vigor and warmth everywhere that it touches me. I breathe it in deeply once more, and instead of the suffocating feelings I previously felt I am content and comfortable. I let the colors wash over me and bathe me in their light.

Slowly the colors mesh and settle and I am looking at an idyllic countryside. My senses are overwhelmed. The smell of trees and grass, the sound of babbling brooks and streams, the dazzling clear blue sky overhead. Mountains stand against the once formless horizon. I look down and see myself floating gently above the inviting lawn of this beautiful wilderness. I look out once more and see animals grazing here and there. Some large, some small, all going about their life in the most earnest manner they can. These animals are not complex, they simply seek to exist, and create progeny to continue their species. There is an honor and righteousness in their simplicity. I regard them with love, simply for the sake of them and what they are.

I smile, and know that I have arrived at my destination. I didn't even know I had a destination before, but this is clearly where I am meant to go. With confidence I let myself settle onto the verdant floor. The grass rises between my toes, and I relish the feeling. This place is truly my peace given form. I look once more to the horizon, and I know everything about this place. I know all the beasts that walk this place, all the plants that grow. I know all the hills, valleys, and peaks. I know all the streams, rivers, and fords. I know what I see now is the past, present, and future. I am here now, and I will never be lost again.

END

Dedicated to my dearest friends,

My parents, children, and family

And all of you who are
struggling out there.

Stay Well.

Thank you

You have finished the book. With all the sincerity I can muster, I am grateful to you. These writings were something I've worked on over the past year, and they have helped me get through many difficulties. I hope they may also offer you some comfort.

\- N. S.